Essentials of Information Literacy and E-Information Literacy for Information Seekers

Essentials of Information Literacy and E-Information Literacy for Information Seekers

PRAKASH BHAIRU BILAWAR
Assistant Librarian (Selection Grade),
Barr. Balasaheb Khardekar Library,
Shivaji University, Kolhapur, Maharashtra, India

Ess Ess Publications
New Delhi

ESSENTIALS OF INFORMATION LITERACY AND E-INFORMATION LITERACY FOR INFORMATION SEEKERS

ISBN : 978-81-934311-5-3

First Published 2018

Published by:
Ess Ess Publications
4831/24, Ansari Road,
Darya Ganj,
New Delhi-110 002.
INDIA
Phones: 23260807, 41563444
Fax: 41563334
E-mail: info@essessreference.com
www.essessreference.com

Cover Design by *Patch Creative Unit*

Printed and bound in India at Yash Printographics.

Dedicated
to my beloved father

LATE SH. BHAIRU PARASHRAM BILAWAR

Contents

Foreword

Information Literacy (IL) revolves around need for information, to be able to locate, retrieve, evaluate and effectively use the information to resolve the issue in hand (*United States National Forum on Information Literacy*). Although, its relation is attributed to other forms of literacies viz. computer literacy, media literacy etc. but, it has emerged has a key literacy for the social and economic well being of an individual. In the advent of digital era influenced to a greater extent by the Internet, it has gained much more momentum to enable individuals to find the right information, from the digital sea of information. It is now often referred as 'E-information literacy' owing to the shift in the format from print to digital. In a way it has become ubiquitous for the lifelong learning.

This book provides valuable insights on information literacy, its standards, models and tools for measuring information literacy skills among individuals. It further extends to the topic of 'e-Information literacy' and its significance in the present digital era. E-information literacy has become very critical in locating, retrieving, evaluating and using the required information. It emphasizes on kinds of information literacy skills in comparison to print and electronic world, thus giving a vibrant picture of skills one need to have to succeed in locating the needed information in the digital world. The author, Dr. P.B. Bilawar has also elaborated on the role of libraries in enhancing the information literacy skills of individuals. He further emphasized on the kinds of activities libraries need to undertake to harness the skill levels of users to independently sustain themselves in the digital world. It also emphasized on the role of national and international organizations in enhancing the information literacy skills. He has gone a step ahead by discussing what should be the futuristic approach to information literacy by taking note of UNESCO's Five Laws of Information and Media Literacy.

Information literacy skill has become utmost important to deal with the complex nature of information. In the new age of digital world, it is necessary to provide information literacy training to students, researchers and practitioners to enable them to successfully retrieve the needed information. This book is a good step in that direction to make LIS professionals learns about the nuances of information literacy and e-information literacy.

Dr. Shamprasad M. Pujar
Deputy Librarian
Indira Gandhi Institute of
Development Research (IGIDR), Mumbai.

Preface

We live in an era of information abundance where everyone has their own ways of acquiring information using the best possible skills and tools at hand. In the process of Knowledge Management, information literacy is basic and relevant for all age groups ranging from primary schools to senior citizens and is a more significant tool for teachers and professionals. E-Information literacy is the natural extension of information literacy which enables proper use and evaluation of electronic resources, tools and services applied in the learning process. The monolithic vision of Information Literacy thus guides the reader towards the authentic and reliable sources of information.

The present book incorporates the essentials of information handling skills/techniques of information literacy and e-information literacy by highlighting the aspects like measuring tools of information literacy skills, practices/ methods tailored by library and information centers in enhancing information literacy/e-information literacy skills, library and teachers collaboration in setting of information literacy programs, role of working organizations in promotion of information literacy with the base of models and standards of information literacy/e-information literacy use for the information seekers. Hence the coverage of the book is very unique and comprehensive.

I think the book would act as a pedagogical basic reference tool for library and information science (LIS) students (UG/PG) and teachers in the LIS subject as it is peculiar towards the aspects of information literacy. I am confident that the students and teachers will find the contents of the book immensely useful for their learning and teaching on information literacy/e-information literacy as a part of their syllabus component.

However, I have taken utmost care to avoid errors/ omissions but some might have escaped my attention. Any sort of suggestions/recommendations for the improvement of the book are always welcome.

— Prakash B. Bilawar

Acknowledgements

I would like to thank Dr. Shamprasad M. Pujar, for his continuous guidance, support and encouragement. His insights, keen observations and valuable suggestions are really appreciated.

I would also like to thank many people for their proper counsel, direction and good wishes which enabled me to complete the book in hand they are Dr. N. I. Divatankar, my teacher and former Head, Department of Library and Information Science, Shivaji University Kolhapur, Dr. Namita B. Khot, Director, Knowledge Resource Center (B.B.K. Library), Shivaji University Kolhapur, my professional colleagues Dr. Y. G. Jadhav, Asst. Professor, Dept. of Library and Information Science, Shivaji University Kolhapur, Dr. D.B. Sutar, Deputy Librarian, B.B.K. Library, Shivaji University Kolhapur and all the staff of B.B.K. Library and Shivaji University authorities for their courteous cooperation and support.

I must also acknowledge the encouragement and moral support I have received from my family members, my mother Shantabai, my elder brother Sanjay, wife Renuka, daughter Swarupa and son Shreesh.

Many many thanks to Mr. Sumit Sethi, Chief Executive and the editorial team of Ess Ess Publications for their unwavering assistance in several aspects and helpful comments in reviewing and bringing out this book in time.

Finally, it was possible by the virtue of my parents, who are the influencing force behind me and my work.

— Prakash B. Bilawar

1
Information Literacy

PREAMBLE

The growth and change of publications patterns, multidisciplinary nature of subjects and users' demand for nascent information has resulted into generation of flood of information in variety of formats/medias. It is available in print, more and more in electronic formats from millions of websites, search engines, social media, institutional repositories, portals and discussion forums on the internet. Today, getting information is easier, but finding and locating useful, relevant and authentic information from a digital sea of information is very difficult. The information literacy skills help in eradicating such difficulties and provide the roadmap for getting right and relevant information.

The main aim of information literacy is to make the individual information literate. It is observed from the late 1980s that there were various programs conducted by different institutions throughout the world to make people more information literate. Once they are information literate evidently they can use and manage information from the vast and varied type of information sources and thus purpose gets fulfilled. Now access is not enough, but practicability to use and retrieval of information is of much importance. In this situation information literacy skills can act as a catalyst to complete the process. In the information literacy process the core focus is on the learning activities rather than teaching activities as the objectives of information literacy are common to all disciplines, learning scenarios and all levels of education.

With the boon of information literacy at all levels now it is recognized as a social and professional necessity. "Information literacy courses tend to concentrate on the acquisition of the types of skills that information professionals themselves possess, and success in this is both superficial and largely unsuccessful, particularly when such skills are not integrated into the mainstream of educational programs" (Myburgh, 2005). The information literate individuals are the self-directed learners, who individually or collaboratively can use, apply relevant and appropriate information to create quality based products and services benefitted for lifelong learning. It helps them to become a lifelong learners by better understanding the effective methods of use of information.

1.1. What is Information Literacy?

The terms such as library instruction, user education/orientation, library research, teaching library and library literacy etc. refers to use of library information, however by the time and with the arrival of internet they were replaced by information competency, information skill, information fluency, information empowerment, information mediacy, information cache, 'information literacy', as well as other forms of literacy, like digital literacy, Information and Communication Technology (ICT) literacy etc. as it has broader perspectives and wider applications than above terms.

The figure given below reflects involvement of different individuals and institutions in information literacy process.

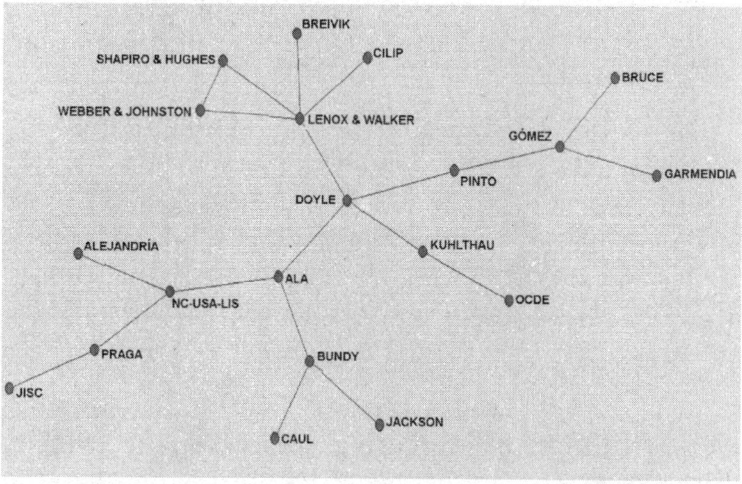

Fig. 1.1. "Interrelationship between the authors and organizations for defining the concept of information literacy" (Uribe, 2009)

Many individuals/organizations/groups have defined information literacy depending upon the perception and use of the concept, since its first mention by Paul Zurkowski in 1974. According to him, "people trained in the application of information resources to their work can be called information literates. They have learned techniques and skills for utilizing the wide range of information tools as well as primary sources in molding information solutions to their problems" (Zurkowski, 1974). More specifically information literacy reflects 'techniques and skills' of information handling for a given problem.

The extensive use of the term 'Information Literacy' was seen in 1989 after the publication of American Library Association's (ALA) final report of the presidential committee on Information literacy. According to ALA Information Literacy is a set of abilities which outlined characteristics of individuals as to "recognize when information is needed and have the ability to locate, evaluate, and use effectively the needed information" (ALA, 1989).

According to Doyle (1992) information literacy "as an individual's ability to; recognize a need for information; identify and locate appropriate information sources; know how to gain access to the information contained in those sources; evaluate the quality of information obtained; organize the information; and use the information effectively."

The above definitions reflect that knowing, identifying, finding, evaluating, organizing, and using of information are the essential key terms and are the requisite skills associated with information literacy.

1.2. Types of Literacies

In the wider sense of scope, tied to technology and culture and use by different groups of users, the term literacy/information literacy has been used as collective term covering various types of literacy's which depends on each other. From the review of literature and available information the conceptual bunch of literacy's is represented in the following diagram in which literacy/ information literacy placed at central place, though the terms ICT Literacy/Digital Literacy correlated with e-information literacy.

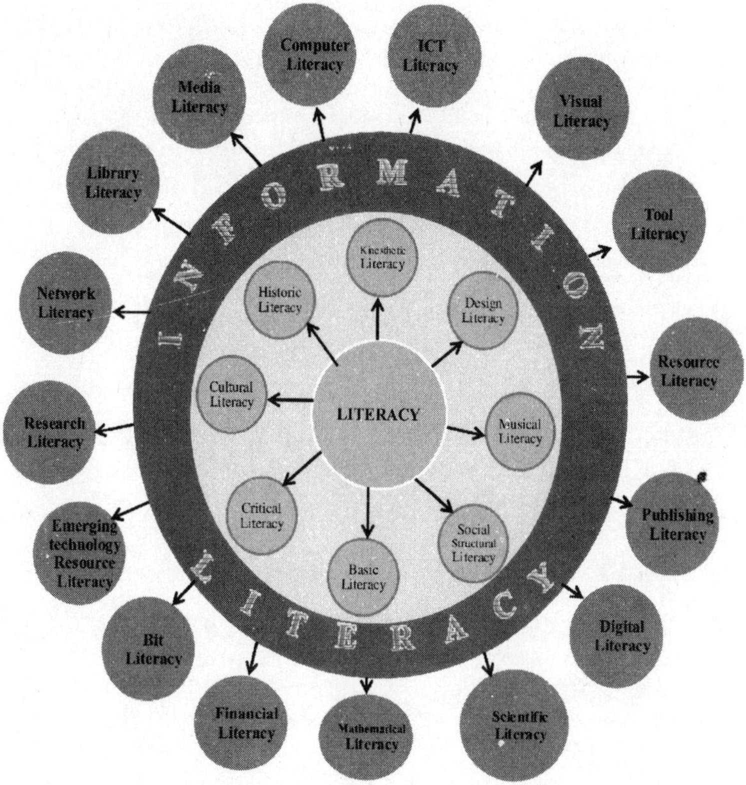

Fig. 1.2. Types of Literacies / Information Literacy

Thus, in wider content information literacy is not bound by single literacy/skill but combinations of several inter related literacy's/skills as shown in above figure 1.2

1.3. Need for Information Literacy

The main aim of Information Literacy is to increase academic performance of stakeholders by exposing, making them aware and use of available library resources independently and encourage them to adopt a stepping stage towards problem solving information techniques.

There is a need of Information Literacy in higher education system owing to following factors-

i. Demand for variety of skills such as technical skills, interpersonal skills and methodological skills for global economy workforce and to survive in competitive world by creating new knowledge and its use in further development process;

ii. To minimize the gap between resources and users and push them in the life long process;

iii. Lack of infrastructure, availability of limited information sources, limited access and working environment;

iv. Uncertain quality and abundant quantity of information in print and digital formats;

v. Applied research on complex and interdisciplinary topics/sub-topics which causes fusion and fission among subject disciplines;

vi. Increase in intake of students strength resulting into poor disorganized and ineffectual use of library and its services;

vii. Changing services/shape of libraries and expansion of library buildings beyond walls;

viii. Rapid curriculum updates and changing demographic interest of students due to socio-economic context;

ix. Realized need for national development;

x. Upgradation of current skills against advances in technology; and

xi. Faculty attitudes

Thus information literacy is the ability to revamp information into knowledge with ethical approach.

REFERENCES

1. American Library Association (1989). *Presidential Committee on Information Literacy*. Final Report. Chicago: American Library Association.

2. Doyle, C.S (1992). *Outcome measure for information literacy within the National Educational Goals of 1990. Final report to the National Forum on Information Literacy*. Syracuse NY: ERIC Clearinghouse on information resources.

3. Myburgh, S. (2005). *The new Information Professional: how to thrive in the information age doing what you love.* England: Chandos Publishing.

4. Uribe, T. A. (2009). Interrelaciones entre veinte definiciones-descripciones del concepto de alfabetización informacional: propuesta de macro-definición. ACIMED. Revista cubana de los profesionales de la información y de la comunicación en salud, 20, n. (Spanish) In Tirado, Alejandro Uribe, Information Literacy Competency Standards for Higher Education and their Correlation with the Cycle of Knowledge Generation, *Liber Quarterly*, 22 (3), 2012.

5. Zurkowski, P. G. (1974). *The Information Service Environment Relationships and Priorities,* Related Paper No. 5, National Commission on Libraries and Information Science, Washington, DC: National Program for Library and Information Services. Retrieved from http://eric.ed.gov/PDFS/ED100391.pdf

2
Information Literacy Models

INTRODUCTION

Lupton (2004) identifies three classes of information literacy models to conceptualize information literacy in educational terms, viz. Standard based, Process based and Relational model. Some of the information literacy models developed by experts and organizations are enlisted below, which can work as information search/process and problem solving models.

- "Kuhlthaus model
- Ellies
- Big 6 Einsenberg and Berkowitz
- Dervin
- Belkin
- SCONUL
- Christine Bruce
- RAC

- Research Cycle
- Alberta Model
- 3 Doors
- SAUCE
- LOUISIANA Model
- Action Learning Model
- Follett's Information Skills Model
- Organized Investigator
- Research Process (Schulz)
- Super 3 Model
- Student Research Guide
- Maland and NCET
- Information Forager" (Lihitkar and others, 2009)
- Loertscher's information literacy model
- The 8 Ws
- Digital Information Fluency Model

From the above enlisted models, the major internationally accepted information literacy models have been discussed below.

2.1. Kuhlthau, Information Seeking Model (1993):

This information search process (ISP) model was developed by Carol Kuhlthau, which depicts users approach and level of confidence towards information (research) processes by directing probable ways of minimizing the negative approaches that occur while undertaking research. It has six step processes applied at different levels viz. Initiation, Selection, Exploration, Formulation, Collection and Presentation.

Generally, task initiation is the first step which is uncertain where needs and priorities are to be defined to accomplish the task followed by selection of possible topic (sources) to overcome the problem. Observing available information on the topic is the third step named as zone of intervention. Predicting and optimizing the foci at a customary level is the fourth turning stage of ISP. The fifth step is compilation of information from different sources/ types of information with searches on the focused topic while the sixth step involves presentation of information in simple and reasoned format.

While reviewing the literature, it is noticed that some of the information sources addressed for the incorporation of final step along with the first six i.e. Assessment to know the outcomes and pitfalls of the entire process.

This model is popular in information seeking flow as it is tested empirically and it is linear in nature.

2.2. Bruce's 7 Faces (1997)

"Christine Bruce (1997) developed a relational model conceptualizing information literacy as seven inter-related faces (components). These seven faces are:

i. Information technology conception;

ii. Information source conception;

iii. Information process conception;

iv. Information control conception;

v. Knowledge construction conception;

vi. Knowledge extension conception; and

vii. Wisdom conception"

The refined outcome statements of the above seven faces have been stated below-

- "Use IT for IR and communication
- Find information independently or via an intermediary
- Use information processes
- Control information
- Build a personal knowledge base in a new area of interest
- Work with knowledge and personal perspectives to gain new insights
- Use information wisely" (Bruce, 2003).

Bruce used the phenomenographic method that attempts to elucidate users envisage the topic rather than their consent about the topic which will help to differentiate the explanation and description concerning their information conceptions. This model is significant as it provides insight framework of information literacy in real sense and assist in understanding the value of information society so that self instructed and self-determined learners will grow up.

The seven faces provide a portrait of information literacy apart from general lists of skills and attributes so that students will get experience to apply these forms of information literacy which is pertinent and specific at different circumstances as each face comprises of unique phenomenon regarding use and apply of 'information'. Thus the outcome of this model is the use of technology for communication of information, the wiser use of information helps to build innovative knowledge in newer area of specialization and execute a scope for development of independent learners by the use and control of information processes.

2.3. Eisenberg and Berkovitz, Big Six Model (1998)

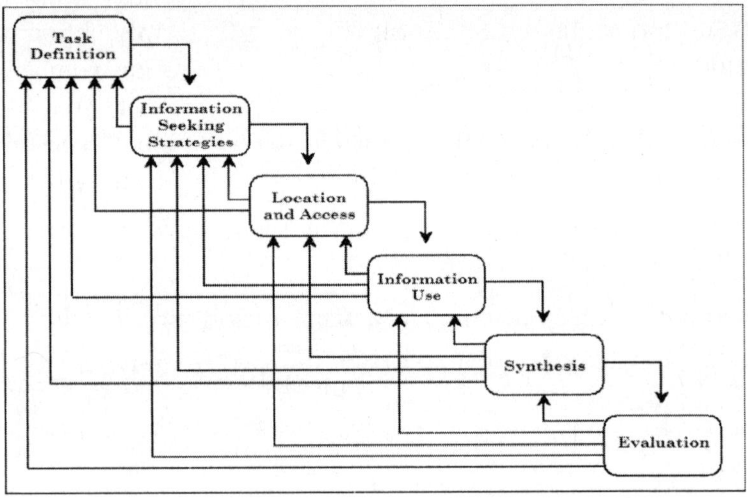

Fig. 2.1. Big Six-Feedback Flow

This model was developed by Eisenberg and Berkowitz in the year 1998. It is a process model in which the information problem is solved by following six steps.

i. Task definition

ii. Selection of information searching strategies

iii. Location and access to resources

iv. Information use

v. Synthesis and

vi. Evaluation

This model helps to identify information seeking priorities, use, pertain and assess relevant information. The key factors are so influencing that the model can be applied at universal level for teaching information and technology skills in a systematic manner and for all age groups.

"Various computer and information technology skills are integral parts of the Big6 Skills. For example, when students use word processing to compose a letter, that's Big6 #5, Synthesis. When they search for information on the World Wide Web, that's Big6 #3, Location & Access. When they use e-mail to discuss an assignment with another student or the teacher, that's Big6 #1, Task Definition" (big6, 2014).

One of the objectives of this model is that it is not necessary to complete the flow in linear order.

2.4. Society of College, National and University Libraries (SCONUL) - Seven Pillar/Seven Faces Model (1999)

This information learning skill model was the outcome of SCONUL paper -Information skills in higher education: a SCONUL position paper. It is grouped into seven stages as shown in Fig 2.2 (SCONUL, 2004).

Later, this model was updated and expanded considering the relevance of different user groups, specialization and ages and then recognized as a 'core' model and 'lenses' model for higher education (Fig. 2.3). The Lenses include:

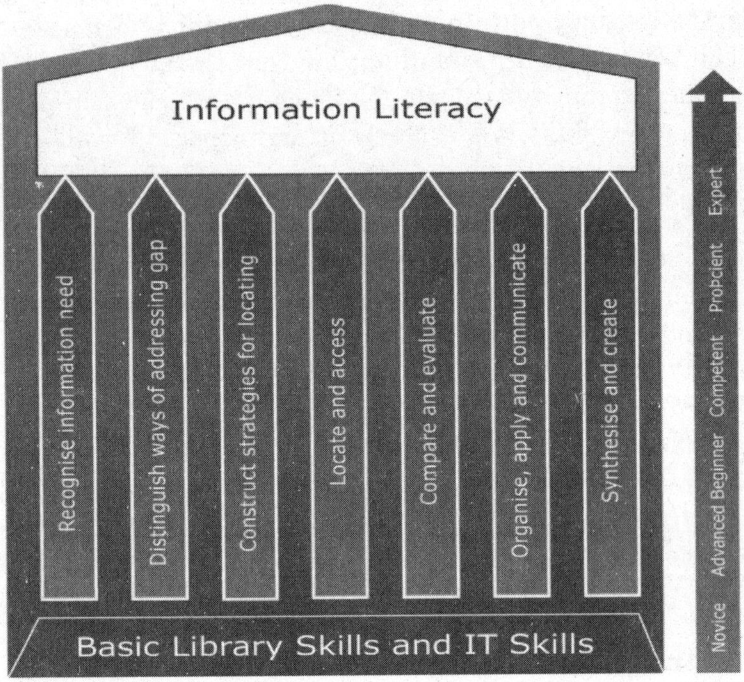

Fig. 2.2. SCONUL Seven Pillars Model for Information Literacy

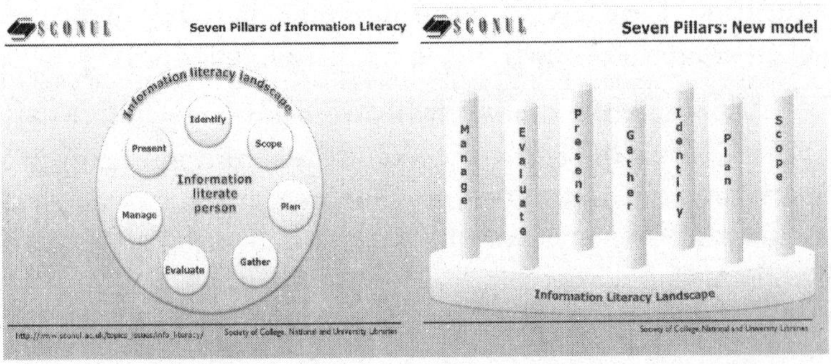

Fig. 2.3. SCONUL: New Models (SCONUL, 2011)

- SCONUL Seven Pillars of Information Literacy: Research Lens

- SCONUL Seven Pillars of Information Literacy: Digital Literacy Lens ; and
- Seven Pillars of Information Literacy: Open Educational Resources Lens

The core model consists of 7 pillars viz. Identify, Scope, Plan, Gather, Evaluate, Manage and Present, which is in resemblance with earlier pillar statements and research lens model.

2.5. Empowering-8 Model (2004)

Empowering-8 model was discussed at an International Federation of Library Associations and Institutions- Action for Development through Libraries Programme (IFLA-ALP) sponsored Information Literacy workshop at National Institute of Library and Information Science (NILIS), University of Colombo, Sri Lanka in the year 2004 and designed especially for Asia-Pacific region for the promotion of information literacy. This model consists of following eight key components as shown in Fig 2.4 :

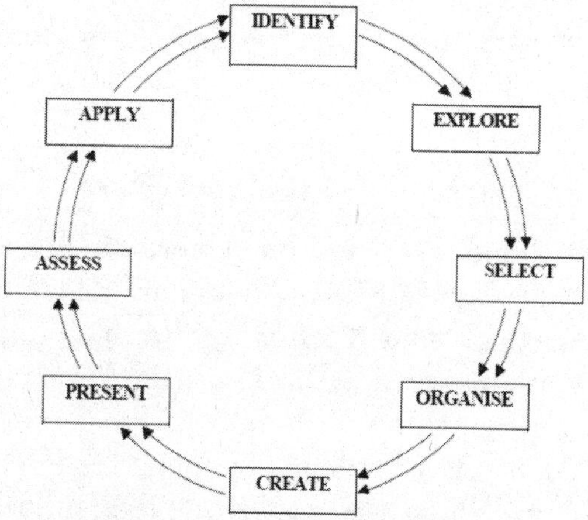

Fig. 2.4. Empowering-8 Model

Russell Bowden (2005) tried to elaborate these 8 steps. Identify a need is the first step to know the subject matter, audience and keywords that will help in understanding a problem. Then 'explore' the problem with available information and resources required to develop search strategy. Based on that 'select' the relevant sources of information that matches with the problem from which information can be obtained or by citing the appropriate sources. Then 'organize' the information from earlier selection which expresses the relation between fact, fiction and opinion. With this 'create' information in one's own words, revise and edit and create bibliography, if required and present this new knowledge in the desired format to share amongst the appropriate audience. 'Assess' the refined new information through feedback, self-assessment and assessment with teachers. Then the last step is applying the generated new knowledge towards next learning activity/problem.

These 8 stages are useful to solve any problem, not necessary to follow the order in a linear way as shown in figure, but entering at one stage followed by subsequent stages to complete the cycle is must. This problem solving endeavor may help at all levels of education and learning scenarios.

2.6. Pathways to Knowledge Model (Pappas/Teppe)

This model is based on American Association of School Librarians (AASL) and Association for Educational Communications and Technology (AECT) information literacy standards. In 1977 Marjorie Pappas and Ann Teppe developed this information process model named as 'Pathways to Knowledge' model. Later on, it was expanded as 'Pathways to Knowledge and Inquiry

Learning' model in 2002. This model is the combination of two perceptions such as inquiry learning and an information process to complete the information search process by the users. It consists of following six stages:

i. Appreciation

ii. Pre-search

iii. Search

iv. Interpretation

v. Communication

vi. Evaluation

Users may continuously explore and reassess at each step as this model is based on non- linear and recursive processes. It is useful to solve information seeking problems and inculcate the students in lifelong learning chain by adopting constricting knowledge techniques.

2.7. Louisiana, Information Literacy Model for lifelong learning

This model provides an intellectual framework in the information search cycle.

It is made of following seven steps and each one of these have been explained below.

i. Defining/Focusing

ii. Selecting Tools and Resources

iii. Extracting and Recording

iv. Processing Information

v. Organizing Information

vi. Presenting Findings

vii. Evaluating Efforts

Defining or focusing the problem by identifying the needs, devise the questions based on nascent information which is particular to the topic and preliminary decisions is the first step. Selecting appropriate 'tools' (search strategy) and 'resources' (print, non-print or digital) focused on the formulated problem is the second step tracked by 'extracting and recording of information'. It includes use of various access and retrieval methods for information processing based on selected tools and sources of information to cover relevant factors. The fourth stage is 'processing' of information with regard to issues of concerns like accuracy, significance, reliability of information and avoids use of ambiguous and wrong information by analyzing the processed information. 'Organizing' the information in lucid and systematic manner by applying critical thinking and problem solving methods to complete a task is the fifth stage of this model followed by 'presentation' of the findings. The task includes use of suitable presentation format, classify the drawn information into suitable type of information and communicate to targeted audience, based on their suggestions corrections can be incorporated. The final stage is 'evaluation' of the task by applying the assessing criteria (self-evaluation, teachers' feedback etc), compliances of the need/research problem, whether new knowledge and skills generated that are going to benefit others. This assists the effectiveness of the whole process. It is the basic model for lifelong learning practices.

2.8. Anderson and Johnston Model

In 2016, Anderson and Johnston designed a general model of information literacy useful for information-using situation consisting of 4 information analysis steps such as person, subject matter, information entity and context bounded in groups of epistemology metacognition critical thinking, epistemology evidence etc, as sketched below-

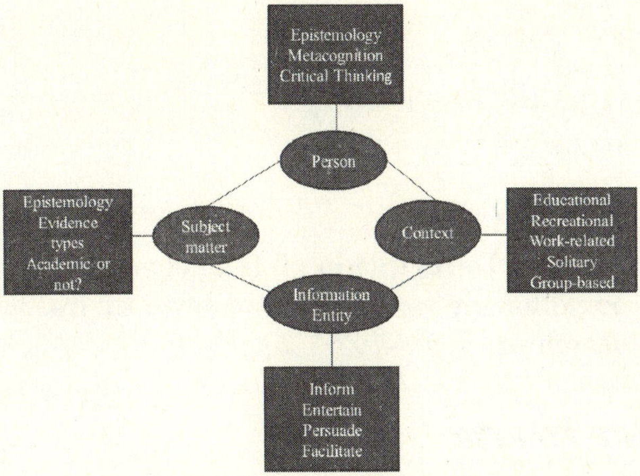

Fig. 2.5. Anderson and Johnston Model of Information Literacy. (Anderson and Johnston, 2017)

2.9. SERVICE : Conceptual Information Literacy Model for Higher Education

From the above it is learnt that the information literacy model consist of range of procedures/stages to complete the flow of information. "The proposed SERVICE Model discussed below is designed considering university library set up, its readers and the terminology from library and information science discipline except the first component STARTER, so that LIS professionals can provide better services to the library users by using simple terminologies from library and information science. The details of the model are as mentioned below:

- **Name :** 'SERVICE' model consisting of seven stages

S STARTER

E ENTRY

R REPOSITORY

V VALIDATION

I INDEX

C CIRCULATION

E EXPLICIT

- **Stages :** Seven
- **Process Description :** It is a network model based on following processes and level of information search process

Stage 1: STARTER

- At the affective level user will approach library with quest in mind and success or failure of quest information

Stage 2: ENTRY

- In the second stage library/staff will expose the resources for selection of information based on quest of user

Stage 3: REPOSITORY

- At the cognitive level user urges to know the location and access for the desired quest of information

Stage 4: VALIDATION

- At the fourth stage user find a suitable source for

his quest after guiding and value (reliable) of acquired information/Search by the library

Stage 5: INDEX

- At the action level user will confirm the information for which quest is made. If it is unsuccessful then repeat the stage

Stage 6: CIRCULATION

- Then the source will be circulated to the inquirer / user

Stage 7: EXPLICIT

- It is the final stage of this process for evaluation, feedback for library from the information seekers.

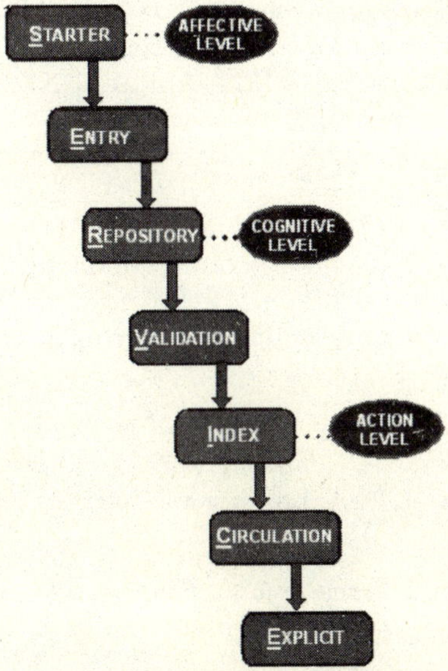

Fig. 2.6. Flow Chart of SERVICE Model" (Bilawar and Pujar, 2011).

This proposed conceptual SERVICE model (Fig. 2.6) aims to work as a gateway for use of different types of information resources by the academicians operational at higher education sector.

REFERENCES

1. Anderson, Tony & Johnston Bill (2017, March), *Critical Thinking, Information Literacy and Epistemological Development: a Webinar*, Views on Information Literacy in Librarianship, Elsevier and Chandos Webinar Series Retrieved from http://scitechconnect.elsevier.com/wp-content/uploads/2017/03/Information-Literacy-Webinar-3-14-final.pdf

2. Big 6, Retrieved from www.big6.com/pages/about/big6-skills-overview.php

3. Bilawar Prakash B, & Pujar S.M (2011, March 2-4), *Information Literacy Models: Correlation and Conceptual Model for Higher Education*. Proceedings of 8th International CALIBER – 2011 sponsored by INFLIBNET Center, Goa: Goa University.

4. Bowden, R. (2005, October 3-7), *Information skills for learning*, Part II. In Empowering 8. Proceedings of International Workshop sponsored by IFLA-ALP and UNESCO-IFAP, Patiala: Punjabi University.

5. Bruce, C. (1997). *The seven faces of information literacy*. Adelaide: Auslib Press

6. Bruce, C. (2003). *Seven faces of information literacy: Towards inviting students into new experiences*. QUT, Retrieved from http://kennison.name/files/zopestore/uploads/libraries/bruce-7-faces.pdf

7. Educational Testing Service (2007). *Digital transformation: a framework for ICT Literacy, A report of the international ICT literacy panel*, USA: Educational Testing Service, 1-42.

8. Lihitkar, S. A. A., & Lihitkar, R. S. (2009, July) Models of information literacy. *Information age*, 3 (3), 29-32.

9. Lupton, M. (2004). *The learning connection: Information literacy and the student experience*. Adelaide: Auslib Press.

10. Picard, C. J. (2004, January). *Guidelines for Library Media Programs In Louisiana Schools*, Louisiana State Department of Education, Retrieved from http://www.louisianaschools.net/lde/uploads/15303.pdf

11. Society of College, National and University libraries (1999). *The seven pillars of information literacy*, Retrieved from http://www.sconul.ac.uk/activities/inf lit/papers/seven pillars.html

12. Society of College, National and University libraries (2011, April). *The SCONUL seven pillars of information literacy, SCONUL working group on Information Literacy*, Retrieved from http://www.sconul.ac.uk/sites/default/ files/documents/coremodel.pdf

13. Society of College, National and University libraries (2004). *Learning Outcomes and Information Literacy*, London: Higher Education Academy.

3

Information Literacy Standards

INTRODUCTION

The Information literacy standards are also referred as components of information literacy. The well known information literacy standards designed by various groups and individuals are mentioned below:

I. Association of College and Research Library's (ACRL): Information Literacy Competency Standards for Higher Education, 2000

II. International Society for Technology in Education (ISTE) Standard: This standard is widely used for learning, teaching in the digital scenario.

III. Australian and New Zealand Institute of Information Literacy (ANZIIL) Standard, 2004: It has six standard viz. Recognize a need for information, Find information, Evaluate information, Manage collected information, Apply prior and new information and Use of information.

IV. American Association of School Librarians And Association for Educational Communications and Technology (AASL And AECT) information literacy standards, 1998

V. Ontario School Library Association (OSLA) information literacy standards

VI. IFLA information literacy standards

Out of above ACRL information literacy standards (components) are very famous and widely used in higher education system. It consists of 5 main standards viz. Determine, Access, Evaluate, Use and Understanding of information (5 Components namely- Identify, Find, Evaluate, Apply and Acknowledge), 22 Performance Indicators (PI) and 87 expected outcomes/skills/knowledge criteria for measuring students learning capabilities. Broadly the ACRL standards are described with their performance indicators and learning outcomes and the same has been detailed below (ACRL, 2000):

Standard One : The information literate student determines the nature and extent of the information needed

The information literate student identifies the need for information by participating in class discussions, peer workgroups electronic discussions. Then he/she consults acquires and classifies the potential sources of information which are available in variety of types and formats relevant to the research topic/need which help in broadening of research topic.

Standard Two : The information literate studen accesses needed information effectively and efficiently

The information literate student selects the mos

appropriate research methodology (e.g., laboratory experiment, simulation, fieldwork etc.), research design and information searching methods/skills (e.g., Boolean operators, truncation, proximity search and search parameters) for accessing the needed information either by online mode or referring reference services and referral sources. Then extracts records and manages the information and its sources.

Standard Three : The information literate student evaluates information and its sources critically and incorporates selected information into his or her knowledge base and value system

The information literate student analyzes the main ideas to be extracted from the information which is gathered from different sources. Assess and compare the information with its reliability, validity, accuracy, authority, timeliness and impact of interpreting the information. Then synthesizes main ideas to construct new concepts and knowledge by using computer and other technologies (e.g. spreadsheets, databases, multimedia, and audio or visual equipment) to explore the interaction amongst the ideas and other phenomena and draws conclusions. If required validates information with other individuals, subject-area experts, and/or practitioners.

Standard Four : The information literate student, individually or as a member of a group, uses information effectively to accomplish a specific purpose

The information literate student applies new and prior information to support the purposes, planning and creation of a particular product or performance (e.g. outlines drafts, storyboards, proper referencing etc). Revises the development process for the product or performance by maintaining log of activities, focusing on past successes, failures and alternative strategies applied and communicate it through ICT media.

Standard Five : The information literate student understands many of the economic, legal, and social issues surrounding the use of information and accesses and uses information ethically and legally

The information literate student understands many of the ethical, legal and socio-economic issues pertaining to information and information technology such as intellectual property, copyright, privacy and security, free vs. fee-based access to information etc. Then uses information ethically and legally without troubling any kind of laws, regulations, institutional policies and etiquette related to the access and use of information resources and acknowledges the use of information sources in communicating the product or performance.

In this standard, revision at each stage within the standard is observed as the common skill.

Recently ACRL released new revised framework on information literacy as 'Framework for Information Literacy for Higher Education' which highlights on 6 frameworks viz. Authority is Constructed and Contextual, Information Creation as a Process, Information has Value, Research as Inquiry, Scholarship is a Conversation and Searching is Strategic. Accordingly the revised definition of information literacy is – "a spectrum of abilities, practices, and habits of mind that extends and deepens learning through engagement with the information ecosystem. It includes

- understanding essential concepts about that ecosystem;

"Table 1. Correlation Between Models of Information Literacy

Model Description	Kuhlthaus Model	Big 6 Einsenberg and Berkowitz	SCONUL Seven Pillars Model(1999)	ACRL	ANZIIL	Pappas/ Tepe Pathways to Knowledge	Louisiana	The Alberta Model	Empowering –8 Model
First Step: INITIATION	1. Initiation	1.Task Definition	1. Recognize information need	1 Determine the extent of information needed	1 Recognize a need for information and determine the extent of Information needed	1. Appreciation	1 Defining/ Focusing	1.Planning Information	1. Identify 2. Explore
Second Step: SELECTION OF RESOURCES	2. Selection 5. Collection	2. Information Seeking Strategies	2. Distinguish ways of addressing gap	3 Evaluate information and its sources critically and incorporate selected information into his or her knowledge base and value system	2 Find information effectively and efficiently	2. Pre-search	2 Selecting Tools and Resources	2.Retrieval Information	3. Select
Third Step: LOCATION, PROCESSING & SEARCH	3.Exploration 4. Formulation	3. Location & Access	3. Construct strategies for locating 4. Locate and access	2 Access the needed information effectively and efficiently	3.Critically evaluate Information and the information seeking process	3. Search	3 Extracting and Recording 4 Processing Information	3.Processing Information	4.Organize 5. Create
Fourth Step: USE OF INFORMATION	6. Presentation	4. Use	6.Organize, apply and communicate	4 Use information effectively to accomplish a specific purpose	4.Manage information collected or generated 6.Use information with understanding and acknowledge cultural, ethical, economic, legal and social issues surrounding the use of information	4. Interpretation	5 Organizing Information	4.Sharing	6. Present
Fifth Step: SYNTHESIS AND EVALUATION	7. Assessment	5. Synthesis 6. Evaluation	5. Compare and evaluate 7. Synthesis and create	5 Understand many of the economic, legal, and social issues surrounding the use of information and accesses and uses information ethically and legally	5 Apply prior and new information to construct new concepts or create new understandings	5. Communication 6. Evaluation	6 Presenting Findings 7 Evaluating Efforts	5.Evaluation	7. Assess 8.Apply
TOTAL STAGES	7	6	7	5	6	6	7	5	8

(Bilawar and Pujar, 2011)"

- engaging in creative inquiry and critical reflection to develop questions and to find, evaluate, and manage information through an iterative process;
- creating new knowledge through ethical participation in communities of learning, scholarship, and civic purpose; and
- adopting a strategic view of the interests, biases, and assumptions present in the information ecosystem". (ACRL, 2014)

3.1. Correlation between Models and Standards of Information Literacy:

Following Table-1 shows comparison between information literacy models, skills and standards formulated by different authorities. Few of the popular models in correlation with others are compared below:

In the above table the steps defined in the column 5 and 6 are the Information Literacy standards of ACRL and ANZIIL and rests are information literacy models of different individuals/organizations.

REFERENCES

1. Association of College and Research Libraries (2000). *Information Literacy Competency Standards for Higher Education.* Retrieved from www.ala.org/ala/acrl/acrlstandards.htm
2. Association of College and Research Libraries (2014). *Framework for Information Literacy for Higher Education* Retrieved from http://acrl.ala.org/ilstandards/?page_id=133
3. Bilawar Prakash B, & Pujar S.M (2011, March 2-4), *Information Literacy Models: Correlation and Conceptual Model for Higher Education.* Proceedings of 8th International CALIBER – 2011 sponsored by INFLIBNET Center, Goa: Goa University.

4. Suriya, M., & others (2009, January-March). Essential information literacy skills of LIS professionals in engineering institutions based on ACRL standards: Need of a study, *SALIS Journal of Library and Information Science*, 1(1), 26-33.

4

Tools for Measuring Information Literacy Skills

INTRODUCTION

In the changing scenario the information literacy is related to information technology skills, in which these skills are interwoven with the support of information literacy. The element information competency is necessary for understanding options, taking fruitful decisions and carrying out informed and creative actions. It is a set of skills and techniques required to perform information handling tasks like- locating, accessing, using and evaluating information effectively and efficiently from different sources of information. Such kinds of competency are in greater demand especially in academics, business, politics, management, entertainment and libraries.

According to Tiwari (2009) "new skills, both generic and specific- are needed to teach information literacy in a global society, skills that were not generally taught in library science and information programs. As the use of new, internationally-based technologies became widespread, the skills and ability to access, evaluate and use meaningful content became ever more important. Librarians would have to take responsibility, along with teaching academics, for providing those skills; but they had to acquire the teaching knowledge before they could teach information literacy skills."

Many universities, organizations, professionals and experts have developed and reported various tools, methods and instruments for measuring information literacy skills. Some of them are:

4.1. The Project — Standardized Assessment of Information Literacy Skills (SAILS)

A group of skill set began in 2001 at Kent State University to develop a standardized test of information literacy skills assessment irrespective of institution/library of all types and sizes. Used item response theory (IRT) as the measurement model by grouping bank of test questions which are based on ACRL standards to assess and guide the level of information literacy of the students.

4.2. The Information Literacy Test (ILT)

It based on ACRL standards useful to assess information literacy competencies of college/university enrolled students. It is a web based test and covers around 60 multiple choice test questions with response alternatives (options) ranges from three to six. Before appearing for the test requisite proctor training needs to complete.

4.3. Information Literacy in Technology Assessment (ILIT)

It meant to assess student's ability to access,

evaluate, incorporate, and use information based on technological aspects. Again it follows ACRL standards as a fundamental standard. It includes combination of multiple choice and performance based questions which then quickly and efficiently tested and expose students' master skills.

4.4. Tool for Real-time Assessment of Information Literacy Skills (TRAILS)

It is a project of Kent State University Library to measure the information seeking skills of school students without charging any fees. The multiple choice questions grouped into five information categories with grades.

4.5. Centre for Information Literacy Research (CILR)

It was developed in 2007 with the intention to develop the research agenda and teaching excellence in the field of information literacy and information behavior. The methodology adopted includes research projects, publications, research events, invited talks and seminars at national and international conferences, and participation in specialist networks and associations for promotion of information literacy.

4.6. Information Literacy Self-Efficacy Scale (ILSES)

It is significant from the research point of view that information literacy makes impact on generic information-based capabilities. The potentials of self-efficacy are measured in terms of scale of certainty that one can perform given task. "Self-efficacy refers to a belief in one's ability to successfully perform a particular behavior or task" (Cassidy and Eachus, 1998). Self-efficacy is categorized into general self-efficacy and task-specific self-efficacy. There is different information literacy self-efficacy scale designed by several individuals and applied it at their work places. Some of them are:

i. Kurbanoglu, A. & Umay (2006) scale is composed of 7 factors and 28 items. "The factors of the scale are determined as defining the need for information, initiating the search strategy, locating and accessing the resources, assessing and comprehending the information, interpreting, synthesizing, and using the information, communicating the information and evaluating the product and process". (Kurbanoglu and others, 2006)

ii. Motivated Strategies for Learning Questionnaire (MSLQ): It was developed to assess university students' motivational orientations and their use of different learning strategies. This scale is composed of 6 factors "intrinsic goal orientation, extrinsic goal orientation, task value, control belief of learning, self-efficacy and test anxiety and 31 items" (Pintrich and others 1991).

iii. Demographic Data: To collect data regarding features of e-learners a form was developed, consist of "Questions related to students' gender, age, type of alma mater, Internet and computer use periods, etc. were included in this form". (Kilic-Cakmak, 2010).

Again the following additional practical components were used to assess information literacy competency and skill by several individuals and institutions -

i. Use of methods like Analysis of bibliographies, Self-assessment, Development of training modules,

Essay, Multiple choice questions, Questionnaire, Observation, Portfolio and reports, Quiz/Test on lessons learned, Simulation, personal assistance, Checklist, Rubrics etc.

ii. iSkills assessment, an Internet based ICT literacy Assessment, developed by Educational Testing Service (ETS)

REFERENCES

1. Cassidy, S, & Eachus, P. (1998). *Developing the computer self-efficacy(CSE) scale: investigating the relationship between CSE, gender and experience with computers* Retrieved from www.chssc.salford.ac.uk/healthSci/ selfeff/selfeff.htm.

2. Chartered Institute of Library and Information Professionals (2012), *Information Literacy Skills* Retrieved from http:// www.cilip.org.uk/sites/ default/files/documents/ Information%20literacy%20skills.pdf

3. Corrall, S. (1998, Winter), Key skills for students in higher education, *SCONUL Newsletter*, 15, 25-29.

4. Kilic-Cakmak, E. (2010). Learning strategies and motivational factors predicting information literacy self-efficacy of e-learners, *Australasian Journal of Educational Technology*, 26(2), 192-208.

5. Kishore A. & Padmaja, M. (2013). Information Literacy skills of the PG students towards the use of electronic information resources: a case study of SVIMS library, Tirupati, In Ramesha Babu (Ed.), *Libraries in the Changing Dimensions of Digital Technology*, Festschrift in honor of Prof. D. Chandran, Delhi: B. R. Publishing Corporation.

6. Kurbanoglu, S.S, Akkoyunlu, B. & Umay, A. (2006). Developing the information literacy self-efficacy scale. *Journal of Documentation,* 62 (6), 730-743.

7. Pintrich, P.R. & others (1991). *A manual for the use of the motivated strategies for learning.* Michigan: The University of Michigan.

8. Tiwari, P. (2009). *Library Evaluation*, New Delhi: APH Publishing Corporation.

9. Uribe, T. A. (2009). Interrelaciones entre veinte definiciones-descripciones del concepto de alfabetización informacional: propuesta de macro-definición. ACIMED. Revista cubana de los profesionales de la información y de la comunicación en salud, 20, n. (Spanish) In Tirado, Alejandro Uribe, Information Literacy Competency Standards for Higher Education and their Correlation with the Cycle of Knowledge Generation, *Liber Quarterly*, 22 (3), 2012.

10. Walsh, A. (2009, March). Information literacy assessment: Where do we start?, *Journal of Librarianship and Information Science*, 41(1), 19-28.

5
E-Information Literacy

INTRODUCTION

With the changing nature and format of information, information literacy is understood as e-information literacy. Information literacy is useful for all types of users; e-information literacy is more significant for e-learners. E-information literacy is the accepted global phenomenon which plays an essential role in fostering adoption and acceptance of digital learning comprises of bundle of networked e-information services. It offers lifelong learning opportunities with stand alone, independent and self-directed learning processes. Moreover, it shifts from "know what" to "knowing how", "how to secure information in changing society". Digital Information Literacy (DIL), e-literacy (eL) and Digital Information Fluency (DIF) etc are the synonymous terms used for e-information literacy.

According to Konappa (2013) "Digital Information Literacy (DIL) is the ability to recognize the need for, to access, and to evaluate electronic information." Nayak & others (2006) define e-information literacy as "the ability to locate, evaluate and effectively use needed information with a set of skills and attitudes for lifelong learning is a product of information society"

Halder (2013) defines e-literacy as, "Computer literacy + information literacy (+ moral or ethical literacy) = e-literacy".

According to Mahapatra (2006) "E-information literacy is the delivery of information, training or education programs via electronic media that includes wide range of electronic communications like Internet, Intranet, satellite broadcast, interactive television, CD-ROM, DVD, audio and video tapes, etc."

Thus, e-information literacy is mainly associated with electronic information management and services, practices, skills and critical thinking by the support of ICT in an electronic environment. In a way, it is a step, next to information literacy.

5.1. Symbiosis between Information Literacy and E-Information Literacy:

In this ever-changing and predominantly digital environment, information literacy is relevant for all ages from primary schools to senior citizens as a channel for lifelong learning and more significant for teachers and professionals. Information Literacy can act as a bridge between library resources/services and the users. Awareness and skills to knob the e-information are the requisite parameter in e-information literacy process. The term symbiosis is used here to exposes the relationship between Information Literacy and E-Information Literacy. Information Literacy is a critical link between knowledge management whereas e-information literacy is the extended form of information literacy with the use of ICT for Knowledge Management (KM), but both are associated with lifelong learning.

Considering the above, it is practical that there is strong relationship between awareness and Literacy (both Information Literacy and E-Information Literacy) in regard to extensive use of information and for KM.

5.2. Why e-information literacy?

There is a need for E-Information Literacy in higher education system because of following reasons:

i. Electronic sources are unfiltered as well as their authority, validity, reliability, accuracy, timeliness, quality and factuality are questioned which pose new challenges for learners in evaluating and understanding as on the face of it, all web pages look alike;

ii. Availability of data in various formats and software/ hardware obsolescence causing difficulty in understanding and accessing leads to 'data smog' and 'digital divide';

iii. Sharpening of skills and expertise, to handle e-information, awareness about significant digital information skills with regard to search strategy, parameters etc are necessary which help in developing extra search skills;

iv. Users' approach towards 24× 7 e-information access as relied on e-sources of Information;

v. Systematic categorization and organization of e-information in a useful and intelligent manner as e-information available in bundled form;

vi. To know the priority and factual e-information based

on demand as lot of irrelevant linked websites open during beginning of search with customization options;

vii. To identify how to make effective search on the internet and to find out the main concept in the related topic i.e. to develop users knowledge and skills in retrieving desired information;

viii. To provide remote, multiuser and timely access, search-efficacy and further links;

ix. Massive use of 'content publishing' (e-publishing) in open access mode on web;

x. Enforcement of ICT in all disciplines, which is global and capable of transcending socio-cultural and language barrier, needs to acquire learning techniques;

xi. Acknowledge and respect towards intellectual property rights/copyright issues, code of ethics and understanding the laws for information security as content may includes categories, keywords, typologies, links, new records, navigability, updates, plenty of info-guides etc. ;

xii. To find, explore, communicate and evaluation of desired e-information; and

xiii. Traditional libraries are not able to cope up the individual interest of user for quest of information and greater scope towards e-information generation.

REFERENCES

1. Chaminda, C. J. (2008). User perceptions and expectations on e-information literacy development programmes: a gap analysis. *ORBIS-Scientific e-journal of Human Science,* 4 (10).

2. Halder, S. N. (2013). *Library and Information Science in Changing Paradigm.* New Delhi: Ess Ess Publications.

3. Konappa, D. (2013). Digital Information Literacy among research scholars in Sri Venkateshwara University, Tirupati (A.P): An analytical study. In Ramesha Babu (Ed.), *Libraries in the Changing Dimensions of Digital Technology*, Festschrift in honour of Prof. D. Chandran, Delhi: B. R. Publishing Corporation.

4. Mahapatra, G. (2006, February 2-4). 'Towards e-information literacy: quest for interoperable web based information system', *4th International Convention CALIBER-2006,* Gulbarga: INFLIBNET Centre, Ahmedabad.

5. Nayak, V.D. & others (2006, 2-4 February). 'E-information literacy: an overview', *4th International Convention CALIBER-2006,* Gulbarga: INFLIBNET Centre, Ahmedabad.

6

Information Literacy/ E-Information Literacy Skills

INTRODUCTION

According to Chartered Institute of Library and Information Professionals (2012), "Skills required to be information literate require an understanding of:

- A need for information
- The resources available
- How to find information
- The need to evaluate results
- How to work with or exploit results
- Ethics and responsibility of use
- How to communicate or share your findings
- How to manage your findings"

There are different types of information skills such as basic, problem solving generic skills, resource management, social skills, system skills, technical skills,

skills for managing libraries, IT skills and online internet information searching skills like formal, strategic, operational, instrumental, structural, searching skills etc. These skills does not come automatically but are acquired systematically either by training or by experience.

Barry (2007) has given comparison between Basic and electronic information skills:

Basic information skills	Electronic world information skills
Formulate and analyze need	Define information need to fit information retrieval requirements
	Focus questions to enhance precision
Identify likely sources	Understanding range of IT systems
	Use browsing alongside traditional retrieval techniques
Local individual resource	Knowledge of how to access
Examine, select and reject sources	Need to apply range of information science techniques
	broadening and narrowing, Boolean Logic, etc
Interrogate sources	Internet navigation skills
	Reading hypertext
Record and store information	Translation of information across interfaces from search system to personal bibliography
Interpret, analyze, synthesize and evaluate information collected	Awareness of how to make quality assessments for material outside the peer review process
Present and communicate	Web page development skills
resulting work	Use of electronic communication for dissemination
Evaluate what has been achieved	Use of discussion lists

The means and methods (skills) of learning in the process of information literacy is expressed in the words of Hortan (2009) as "Over the course of your lifetime, the more you learn and thereby come to know, but especially the sooner you master and adopt proficient learning skills, habits and attitudes - finding out how, from where, from whom and when to search for and retrieve the information that you need to know, but have not yet learned - the more information literate you thereby become. Your competency in applying and utilizing those skills, habits and attitudes will enable you to make sounder and timelier decisions to cope with your personal and family health and welfare, educational, job-related, citizenship and other challenges. The core idea in the above paragraph is the equating of the Information Literacy concept to learning to learn."

For acquiring information, getting awareness about information tools, for building search strategies and searching skills, understanding the various types of skills and competencies is essential, which are elaborately discussed below as it is required for the effective searching and in e-information literacy process.

6.1. E-information access skills and techniques

Following are the essential e-information skills useful while acquiring e-information:

- Accessing e-resources linked through library website;
- Always ask help from the librarian or teacher in finding the requisite information and using the web strategy ;
- Always keep in mind that whatever available on net is not free;
- Always refine the search as and when necessitates ;

- Application of other searching features such as Stemming search, Fuzzy search, Phonetic search, Case sensitive/intensive, range searching, preference, cluster, snowball , letter replacement, expert searching and visual search interface so as to achieve 'search-efficacy';
- Avoid retrieving of too much of e-information and irrelevant simultaneously;
- Avoid use of same search engine;
- Before applying search technique for a title/quest, it is necessary to find out the source of information i.e. organization tentatively where this quest belong, then trace out the type of organization (commercial agency, company, organization, academic institution etc) to show a domain name. After that propose apt Uniform Resource Locator (URL) depends upon organization and its type or make use of subject directories which explore right information. These steps help the learners to find out relevant and good quality e-information for the desired quest/enquiry;
- Browsing content from E-Print archives/Digital Library/Institutional Repository for preparing assignments, syllabus, lecture presentation etc.;
- Application of relevant, related phrase and rephrasing of the query whenever required;
- By browsing e-Journals/Databases, websites etc for thematic search by applying date, subject, language, format and type of limits to searches;
- By federated searching (parallel searching) options which explores all subscribed and free e-resources simultaneously;

- By just entering the keywords/title/author in simple search box;
- By making search for content within specific domains (.edu, ac.in, co. in etc);
- By making use of mathematical operators [+, -, *] along with keywords;
- Create bookmark of favorite, consistently used web tools;
- Development of own skills, useful to identify effectively the gaps in learners skills;
- Directly going to source of information (Knowing web address from references);
- Evaluative criteria applied for web sources with regard to validity, accuracy, comprehensiveness, uniqueness, navigation ease, standards applied, particulars about composition and organization, user support, search capabilities and type of search, content coverage links, response time, up gradation and integrity factor, availability of index, notes, bibliography, illustrations, multimedia etc.;
- Use of features such as drag and drop, image resizing, spellchecker, style wizard, multilingual content support, FAQ, response time, link, Suffix-Prefix etc needs to be confirmed while using e-resources/contents;
- Going behind first screen as to meet the defined information on a topic;
- Knowledge about searching skills like formal, strategic, operational, instrumental, structural skills etc.;

- Links to abstract, links provided in e-mail table of contents alerts, Full Text, Citation (reference) and other useful e- resources in the field;
- Make use of Advance search options and Boolean operators (and, or and not) along with keywords;
- Making search for content within specific languages (English, Hindi, French etc);
- Making search for content within the files (PDF, HTML, DOC, XLS etc);
- Making use of general search engines, guided Search/ FAQ/Help, Meta Search Engines, Scholarly Search Engines, Subject specific search engines and other search engine applications ;
- Must know the limitations of search engines;
- Noting the fact that general purpose search engines offer free access whereas databases may be free or fee-based access;
- Referring back-of-book indexes;
- Regularly attend appropriate training sessions to keep up to date and participating in e-mail discussion lists, bulletin boards and other such online forums;
- Remember the path of searching from one link to another if lost the learners are of the mind that no information is available on a topic and quit the task;
- Search for articles using Journals database Search options (open access/licensed) and Abstracting and Indexing Databases ;
- Through library OPAC (Article Indexing);
- To keep preferring access against the quality and need;

- To know when to quit as related and useful information is made available at first screen or the next. Depending upon the usefulness of searched information quit the task it saves enormous amount of time while browsing;
- To understand, compare, combine, annotate, and apply the retrieved information using appropriate software's such as spreadsheet, database, statistical and reference management tools etc for better exploitation of results;
- Use of phrase/exact word search by putting content in and proximity operators (near, between etc.);
- Use of subject directories/gateways/web index and Subject bookmarking sites;
- Use of web/internet indexing techniques for e-information; and
- Watching video lectures from academic/research organization (Ex: You tube)

6.2. Web based information skills and E-information skills

It is a perfect mixture of practical skills for handling of ICT with e-resources and formation of novel moderate skills for fair use of e-information. As per the definition of e-information literacy it directs towards information seeking behavior skills of the users. It includes skill to use effective search technique in search engines, skill to use internet for accessing e-resources, collection development, research and learning activities and referencing , skills to develop digital library, institutional repositories, portals and library automation, tools and techniques of data warehouses, data mining and knowledge discovery in databases and skill to use storage media etc.

Further, it covers the areas like Indexing and Abstracting, Application of taxonomy and Controlled Vocabulary Development, Networking and community outreach, Faceted Web mining, Communication and presentation skills and Standards and patents.

6.3. ICT skills

According to Corrall (1998) IT skills include:

- "Basic skills (use of keyboard, mouse, printer, file/ disk management)
- Standard software (word processing, spreadsheets, databases, etc.)
- Network applications (electronic mail, Internet, web browsers)"

Apart from that it includes knowledge of database management, online access management, web page design, networking, handling of digital resources and exchange of data as per standard.

6.4. Information skills/Information handling skills

Information skills has broader approach than ICT Skills as it is directly linked with generation and analysis of knowledge which is most frequently used component in higher education and society in general. It includes the task like sources of information, evaluation criteria, navigation methods, manipulation and presentation techniques, Reflective Online Searching Skills (ROSS) and fluency with ICT etc.

6.5. Library skills

"Library skills can be divided in two categories: *transferable* and *specific*. The transferable library skills are those skills that can be used in any library: strategies of searching information in an online catalogue, how to use a reference work etc. The specific library skills refers to the way the library is organized (i.e. what type of publications are available on open shelves, what type of organizing criteria is used in that library, the way that knowledge domains are displaced in study rooms, which is the destination of the study rooms-for books/serials/ audiovisual documents etc.), classification system used, available services, eventual costs involved in offering those services" (Coravu, 2010).

6.6. Social networking skills

The skills driven in accessing social networking includes interacting(connecting) with group patrons within the sites, updating with new contacts/profiles and new information, creating and dissemination of content in multimedia form, displaying announcement/views/ opinion/chatting and evaluation on a particular topic, searching and navigating the information.

6.7. Other skills and sources

Certain other skills and sources need to be applied to get additional and related information, some of such skills include the following:-

Cyberabstracts

It is an academic digital open source portal recently developed as a best abstracting service, which provide links to the reference, abstract, keywords, assessment and full text access etc. "*Cyberabstracts* is an academic initiative addressed to the higher/further education community (students, teachers and researchers) as a specialized set of quality resources on information analysis and representation: it constitutes a laboratory that allows for in-depth learning of the informative skills and competencies, and is mainly centered on information analysis and evaluation" (Pinto, 2008).

Power browsing and Concept Mapping

The term was introduced by British Library in the Ciber briefing paper, to depict the technique of accessing the e-information. "Power browsing is skimming websites, scanning indexes, reading the first page of an article and downloading reports in great amount" (British Library , 2008).

Concept Mapping is one of the imperative e-learning strategies in which concepts are linked, manipulated to other formats in a pattern that best represents the meaningful information through the use of computers. "They can be beneficially applied in teacher education programme, other educational context for planning instruction, for presenting learning content, as a learning strategy for individual learners and groups as well as for assessing knowledge and tracking changes in knowledge, practical knowledge of mentor teachers in teacher education programme" (Rai and Dvivedi, 2010). The next landmark in this area is Knowledge Map (K-map).

REFERENCES

1. Barry, C. A. (1997, June), Information skills for an electronic world: training doctoral research students, *Journal of information science*, 23(3), 225-228.

2. British Library (2008). *A Ciber briefing paper, information behavior of the researcher of the future*. London: Ciber, British Library.

3. Chartered Institute of Library and Information Professionals (2012), *Information Literacy Skills* Retrieved from http://www.cilip.org.uk/sites/ default/files/documents/Information%20 literacy%20skills.pdf

4. Coravu, R. (2010, April 21-23). Library literacy: the step before information literacy, *First international conference in Romanian on Information Literacy*, E-Lis: Romania.

5. Corrall, S. (1998, Winter), Key skills for students in higher education, *SCONUL Newsletter*, 15, 25-29.

6. Horton, F. W. (2009). Information literacy and learning to learn, In Jagtar Singh, etal. (Ed.) *Library and Information Science in Digital Age,* Essays in honor of Professor M.P.Satija, V.1, New Delhi: Ess Ess Publication. P-117-119.

7. Pinto, M. (2008, April). Cyberabstracts: a portal on the subject of abstracting designed to improve information literacy skills, *Journal of Information Science* 34 (5), 667-679.

8. Rai, R. & Dvivedi, S. (2010, August 9-15). Concept Mapping as a technological tool to facilitate teacher education programme and enhance e-learning, *University News*, 48 (32), 14-17.

7
Role of Library and Information Centers in Enhancing Information Literacy and E-Information Literacy Skills

INTRODUCTION

The role of library and information centers in promoting information literacy amongst the users is decisive. Considering variety in readers' category, their discipline and trend towards e-learning oriented services, library and information centers should organize various programs such as user awareness, hands on training sessions, workshops and demonstration on information products and services. This will help in creating awareness and use of advanced electronic library services/facilities and to use the library resources effectively. "University libraries are the major learning channel with important roles to support the educators' teaching and students' learning, particularly in supporting worthwhile and efficient use of information sources. It is extremely necessary for educators and students, who have to conduct research and use information sources by searching or retrieving information from the library, to know and understand information literacy" (Maitaouthong and others, 2012). While implementing information literacy programmes, equal participation of all the stakeholders is essential for the overall success. The librarian has to consider information literacy as a core activity in the academic vicinity. Adequate ICT infrastructure, help desk , positive contribution of higher authorities, merging of qualitative/informative contents and proper mentoring are the essential obligations while running the fruitful e-information literacy programs at the university level.

The role of library and library professionals for the promotion of information literacy/e-information literacy includes the following:

- Development and hosting of tutorials on the use and access of e-resources and other related e-information for all on the library website;
- Development of information searching course as a part of Information Literacy Program (ILP)/ Information Literacy Instruction (ILI) and institutional training;
- Support and arrange soft skill development programs for teachers;
- Addressing changes observed in user behavior and library services through the methods like lecture, hands-on-approach or online sessions;
- Launching of dedicated e-information literacy websites/portal and information literacy laboratory;

- Design and development of IT (Information Technology) zone at Library to browse e-content/e-resources;
- Provision of relaxed reading carrels for academicians;
- Try to overcome diversity in learning styles;
- To encourage, support and nudge users in establishment of their learning priorities and incorporate them in information literacy teaching by providing most inviting and accessible information environment;
- Acts as Information Literacy Educator and E-learning Liaison Librarian;
- Tendency about creating new knowledge through filtering, summarizing and packaging of e-information;
- Awareness and implementation of 'information literacy standards' meant for higher education;
- Be a promoter of new products and services;
- To make a track on online information sources of different disciplines and its availability through Table of Content (TOC), Content Page Alert Service (CPAS), Documents Delivery Service (DDS) or Inter Library Loan (ILL) etc.;
- Be part of faculty meetings to align library collections to users' needs;
- Build deep sense about copyright issues, Intellectual property rights and knowledge management in the minds of users;
- Manage to assess information self-efficacy/efforts of users;

- Has ability of effective handling of technologies like network technology and its services (creation of information literacy network), Artificial Intelligence, Expert system, Data warehousing etc.;
- Updating of library website/web portals and web related services at regular intervals;
- To attend conferences, seminars, workshops regularly in both LIS and other disciplines to improve/update skills and research trends in variety of subjects; and
- To identify user perceptions and expectations on information literacy/ e-information literacy development programmes and to provide e-information services.

7.1. General practices of Libraries in promoting Information Literacy/E-information Literacy

The tasks undertaken by libraries in strengthening of information literacy/e-information literacy are highlighted on the following lines:

- Informing about latest e-resources and other information services through circular, e-mail alert service and news alert on library website;
- Organization of periodic discipline based specific orientation programs, workshops, training, user awareness programs on e-resources/ reference management tools, seminars and conferences with hands on approach schedule for all the stakeholders. The key programs are:
  * Arrangement of Virtual Library Tour

* Arrangement of varied tailored program for teachers
* Building a massive awareness programme on range of topics like citations, webliography, impact factor, search engines, evaluation and use of information/plagiarism and e-resources etc
* Demonstration of use of databases/software (Open Source, Licensed), statistical packages and on Web tools like Zotero, Mendeley etc
* Orientation program on online search and retrieval of information using search engines and CD/Online databases
* Scheduling of interactive online tutorials/ courses
* Course/program feedback and evaluation; and
* Arrangement of information literacy classes/ sessions.

Libraries need to take support from various agencies like union and state governments, local self governments, educational administrators, business houses, industries and NGO's to build a strong rapport for better development of information literacy and its programs and to overcome the impediments observed during the flow of information.

Thus, the role of library is not restricted to educate the users but beyond educating exposes the advantages of emerging new technology to fulfill their learning assignments.

7.2. Faculty-Library collaboration in Information Literacy process

In this era of fierce competition, both teachers and librarians should be 'info-literate' to meet the curriculum aspects of the students. "Faculty-Library collaboration paves the way to make students information literate and finally to make them life-long learners. In traditional universities, the faculty-library collaboration is an emerging phenomenon as these two entities are driven by separate agendas: teaching and providing services. Rapid development in information and communication technologies has built a platform for these two institutions to work collaboratively and for making synergies" (Wijayasundara, 2008).

Collaboration between both of them is equally important for building up information and learning skills and to discover the ways to integrate the course structure and shaping the students in right direction. Library staff needs to build collaborative relationship with faculty members by encouraging and supporting them in information literacy process by incorporating information literacy skills into their teaching and become more information-savvy. "The internet gives so much information, that it can appear much less complicated than it really is. Students, who have no idea how information is indexed, how to use controlled vocabulary, differences between an index and a web search engine, are at present disadvantaging themselves. To put it another way: they don't know what they don't know" (Godwin, 2005). For better collaborative practices and efforts amongst the faculty members and library/librarian the areas needs to be identified which include information skills, research strategy/methodologies in research, e-information skills, presentation skills and managerial skills etc. The improvement in collaboration will cover areas like learning/teaching techniques, arrangement of training programs, information literacy courses etc. by forcing the librarians to work with the faculty in the classroom environment. This collaboration ultimately provides an opportunity to create library instruction program uniquely suited to all individual class needs. Faculty help is very necessary while producing policy documents on information literacy plans/strategic plans and actions.

Regarding the librarian's role in teaching and pedagogical practices, Slavin (2006) used the term 'international teacher'. "He explains that International teachers are those who are constantly thinking about outcomes they want for their students and about how each decision they make moves (students) towards those outcomes."

Therefore librarians need to concentrate on academic perceptions, diffusion and interest for teachers' development in information literacy process with student centric approach.

7.3. Librarian as a Collaborator

The Librarian will work as core collaborator in Faculty Development Programme (FDP) of teachers by creating collaborative environment at the teacher's desk. He need to work as mentor, expert, professional leader and peer rather than information expert in the research and extension accomplishments of the teachers. Further, support higher quality research/project of the faculty members to recognize the research at international level. While pursuing different types of task related to academics and research, teachers demand pertinent and suitable sources of information and it is the foremost duty of LIS professionals to expose them to relevant and improved literature of review towards teachers' research work and support towards curriculum design/revision based on changing scenario. To know the problems faced by the teachers regarding acquiring information or any such setbacks, librarians need to keep continuous contact with the faculty, understand the difficulties and try to overcome the problem.

In this Google era lot of e-information through different sources is available so librarian can guide teachers in regard to web based sources and services and retrieve external resources through inter library loan required for their work. In addition to this, librarian may help in citation management, development of assignment, publications, conference presentation and scientific communication of the teachers to dawn new ideas. Be interested in faculty research, aware about research schemes/collaboration and to guide them while writing research proposals/reports in the required format and language. In this connection librarian need to work as introducer, e-research information consultant, counselor, catalyst, linker, co-teacher, an intelligent agent and facilitator for faculty research and intermediary in the cycle of scholarly communication as many faculty are unaware about existing sources of information and searching/accessing techniques. Further, to identify and use computer skills with faculty member's subject knowledge to meet the faculty research, consultancy, teaching and learning requirements. In nutshell Librarian provide reliable, impactful tools and guidance with regard to handling of information for the benefit of faculty members.

In the teaching-learning process, both faculty and librarian shares teaching responsibility, as faculty delivers the content whereas librarian delivers the sources of information. So, relevant skills useful for handling of information sources are equally imparted to both for carrying out their academic and research pursuits.

7.4. Methods adopted for Information Literacy/E-Information Literacy by Libraries

Following routine practices (methods) in terms of **instructional strategy** are necessary for better use of information resources, to learn constructively and to construct learner's knowledge using information wisely and orienting the users in information literacy process.

- Analogical storytelling is an interaction approach that connects the powerful cognitive processes of individual storyline to facilitate it's meaning-making and help to personalize better librarian-student interactions in the teaching learning process (Johnson, 2008) ;
- Process-Oriented Guided-Inquiry Learning (POGIL) is an extended means of teaching method where student can learn through group interaction and problem solving tactic based on constructivist ideology (Mitchell and Hiatt, 2010);
- Arrangement of Search strategies, tools and resources (ST & R) programs/course/lectures/ seminars and demonstrations in time limit say 45 minutes per program followed by test and results and distribution of e-certificate;
- Arrangement of Virtual Field Trips (VFTs);
- Audio Visual aids such as videos, audio podcasts, slideshows etc.;

- Case studies and success stories;
- Display of Library map and floor-plans;
- Distribution of library manual/brochure/pamphlet/ workbooks etc.;
- Group Discussion/Discussion board/coliaborative learning sessions with other participants;
- Hands-on workshop on digital information literacy competency development programs;
- Information literacy quiz/game and worksheet practical's;
- Library orientation/induction program/sessions/User education program and bibliographic instruction to know library vision, sub-sections and its working, resources, services and facilities, rules and regulation, Library website and portal, calendar, other library information, etc.;
- Library Publicity and Library demonstration;
- Library visits and individual instructions, counseling and personal assistance and instruction (One-on-one instruction);
- Online library course/tutorials like Learning Management Systems (LMS); Course integrated projects, stand-alone courses and Assignment Building;
- Online Training and Web-based seminar (Webinars): Elsevier training desk provide maximum video tutorials as a training resources on variety of subjects, Use of live interactive training;
- Problem-based Learning (PBL) approach motivate the students to accomplish research by integrating

theory and practice and applying skill and knowledge to develop practicable solution to the defined problem;

- Short training programme and co-teaching;
- Universal Design for Learning (UDL) Principle which explore the universal design plan that helps the stakeholders to meet the diverse learning styles rather than documented activities;
- Use of Digital teaching toolbox (developed by San Diego State University for educators);
- Use of multimedia products and services, OPACs and Public Information Kiosks (PIK)/ Talking kiosks through Computer Assisted/Aided Instructional (CAI) programs; and
- User interaction and Interviews (pre and post test/ search).

While running above instructional strategy, time limit for each activity needs to be fixed. Further librarian-faculty collaboration in conducting above strategy is an effective way to improve the program and student learning.

REFERENCES

1. Godwin, P. & Parker, Jo. (2008). *Information Literacy meets Library 2.0*, London: Facet publishing.
2. Johnson, A. M. (2008). Analogical storytelling as a strategy for teaching concept attainment, In Cook Douglas and Sittler Rayan L. *Practical pedagogy for Library Instructors: 17 Innovative Strategies to improve student learning*, USA: American Library Association.
3. Maitaouthong, T. & others (2012, April). The roles of university libraries in supporting the integration of information literacy in the course instruction, *Malaysian Journal of Library & Information Science*, 17 (1), 51-64.

4. Mitchell, E. & Hiatt, D. (2010, November) Perspectives on...Using POGIL Techniques in an Information Literacy Curriculum, *The Journal of Academic Librarianship,* 36 (6), 539–542.

5. Slavin, R. E. (2006). *Educational Psychology: Theory and practice*, Boston: Pearson.

6. Wijayasundara, N. D. (2008). Faculty-library collaboration: A model for University of Colombo, *The International Information and Library Review*, 40, 188-198.

8

Value of Working Organizations in Promotion of Information Literacy Initiatives in India

INTRODUCTION

For super flow of requisite information/e-information promotional activities should be rendered by organizations and institutions. It is noticed that there are different types of organizations working at national and international level valued for intensification of information literacy, its skills and programs in one or the other way.

8.1. List of organizations working at national/ international level for promotion of Information Literacy

Few of the well known contributions from different organization/institutions/universities operational for endorsement of information literacy are enlisted below:

(a) American Association of Higher Education (AAHE)

(b) American Association of School Librarians (AASL)

(c) American Library Association (ALA)

(d) Association of College and Research Libraries (ACRL)

(e) Association for Educational Communication and Technology (AECT)

(f) British Library Development Studies (BLDS)

(g) Chartered Institute of Library and Information Professionals (CILIP)

(h) Educational Testing Service (ETS)

(i) Information Society of Technology in Education (ISTE)

(j) International Federations of Library Associations and Institutions (IFLA)

(k) International Technology Education Association (ITEA)

(l) National Commission on Libraries and Information Science (NLIS)

(m) National Forum on Information Literacy (NFIL)

(n) Project Information Literacy (PIL)

(o) United Nations Educational, Scientific and Cultural Organization (UNESCO)

8.2. Initiatives taken in India for promotion of Information Literacy

"Research institutes, Universities, IITs and International organization like UNESCO etc has taken a fruitful collaborative initiatives for restoring roots of information literacy widely and creates awareness of information literacy amongst their stakeholders called to be 'a great deal of help'.

Few of the initiatives taken in India by various organizations/agencies/schools and institutions for promoting information literacy/e-information literacy are discussed below-

i. 'Saakshar Bharat Mission 2012' a version of 'National Literacy Mission Authority (NLMA) launched by Government of India for promoting education literacy for adults in all states corroborating with SLMA (State Literacy Mission Authority) in each state, districts, block and gram panchayats of the state. Every year '8th September' this day was observed as 'International Literacy Day';

ii. In this line, Senthilkumaran traced that National Institute of Information Technology (NIIT) took the initiatives to launch World Literacy Day (WLD) on December 2nd every year since 2001 to reduce digital divide.;

iii. Formation of National Knowledge Commission (NKC) in 2005 and National Knowledge Network (NKN) in 2010 for mounting 21st Century India into knowledge society;

iv. In line with ERNET (Educational Research Network), EDUSAT India's first dedicated education satellite was launched in 2004. Similarly Vidya Vahini an IT-enabled education project in 2002 and development of open distance network- National Open and Distance Learners Library and Information Network (NODLINET) gives a new dimension towards information needs of distance learners;

v. According to Abraham and Dubey, during next two decades, various functional organizations and movements like *Gram Shiksha Mohim* (Village Education Campaign), Farmers Training and Functional Literacy Project (FTFLP), *Churcha Mandals, Mahila Mandals, Krishi Vigyan Kendras, Shramik Vidyapeeth, Nehru Yuvak Kendra*, Satellite Television Experiment (SITE) and family and child welfare projects were set up ;

vi. Role played by publishers and producers of electronic foundations, in consultation with academic bodies, library/professional associations working at regional, state, national level, societies and national/library networks in encouraging information literacy amongst intellectual masses by the ways of conference, seminars, trainings, workshops, proceedings etc. for information literacy movement at the national and international level.

e.g. In the 51st conference of ILA (Indian Library Association) held on 2005, recommends to form National Information Literacy Mission and a Information Literacy Task Force;

vii. In Maharashtra, as per the directives of Joint Board of Vice Chancellor (JBVC), during the met of Librarians of the Universities in the state it was decided to include Information Literacy component in each course of the LIS curriculum;

viii. Agricultural college and university libraries in India offer teaching course on information skills component in their curriculum of PG and UG courses (credit/elective/short course pattern). The first effort in this direction was taken by Indira Gandhi Krishi Vishvidhalaya, Raipur in 1970;

ix. Academic Staff College approved by University Grants Commission (UGC) conducting regular orientation/refresher course for teachers and librarians to learn in accessing the information. UGC developed the course content of such programs based on ICT mode;

x. Arrangement of program on 'literature search' initiated by National Informatics Center (NIC);

xi. Organizations like National Council of Educational Research and Training (NCERT) / State Council of Educational Research and Training (SCERT) of each state conduct regular orientation/refresher courses for the school librarians regarding awareness and use of information literacy;

xii. The major initiatives has been taken by Navodaya Vidyalayas in which VIth and XIIth class students has to prepare a project report using information resources and IT to enable learning process;

xiii. Akshaya e-literacy program of Kerala state and Maharashtra Knowledge Corporation Ltd. (MKCL) of Maharashtra state initiated Maharashtra state-Certificate in Information Technology (MS-CIT) course to strengthen IT literacy program/course;

xiv. IIT-Kanpur has developed Brihaspati, an open source e-learning platform;

xv. Baskaran pointed out regarding establishment of the national documentation centers like National Institution of Science Communication and Information Resources (NISCAIR) and National Social Science Documentation Centre (NASSDOC) play a significant role in orienting library and information science professionals of the country to acquire the skills of access to information. Apart from that, Developing Library Network (DELNET), Documentation Research and Training Centre (DRTC) and many such government agencies playing a significant role in orienting professionals by conducting IT training programs by delivering the skills of access and retrieval of information on regular basis;

xvi. In 1984, Government of India initiated a Project – CLASS (Computer Literacy And Studies on Schools) for computer literacy. In this connection Ramana added that under this project, the computer literacy has become compulsory for Class XI and XII. It was a step towards e-information literacy in Indian environment;

xvii. Development of e-resource consortia's like Information and Library Network (INFLIBNET) – Infonet Digital Library Consortium, Indian National Digital Library in Engineering Sciences and Technology (INDEST) consortia, Council of Scientific and Industrial Research (CSIR) consortia etc;

xviii. Launching of 'Rashtriya Computer Literacy Drive' (RCLD) to make India 100% computer literate;

xix. IT policies designed and adopted by various states for efficient use of e-information." (Bilawar, 2015).

REFERENCES

1. Abraham, A. & Dubey, J. P. (2013, April-June). The road to literacy: a reality check, *Indian journal of adult education*, 74 (2), 73-84.

2. Baskaran, C (2011, October 10-16). Information Literacy expertise: a preliminary technique on knowledge accomplishment in academic society. *University News,* 49(41), 6-10.

3. Bilawar Prakash Bhairu (2015, July). Role of working organizations in promotion of Information Literacy initiatives in India, *Vishwawarana National Research Journal*, 2 (2), 6-9.

4. Ramana, Y. V. (2005, January 27-29). *Status of e-learning in India,* 23rd Annual convention and conference SIS-2005, Andhra University,Vishakhapatnam.

5. Senthilkumaran, P. (2011, June). Information literacy Programs in India, *SRELS Journal of Information Management.* 48 (3), 357-363.

9

Futuristic Approach towards Information Literacy/ E-Information Literacy

INTRODUCTION

Taking into consideration the importance of information literacy and e-information literacy in the processing cycle of information management it is high time to put theses concept in the augmented reality. So the differential concepts like Critical thinking/brainstorming and information literacy, big data and e-information literacy etc. have taken their position. In this line UNESCO has come out with five laws of Media and Information Literacy (MIL) at par with the five laws enunciated by Dr. S.R. Ranganathan.

9.1. Five Laws of Media and Information Literacy (MIL)

The 5 laws designed by UNESCO are summarized below-

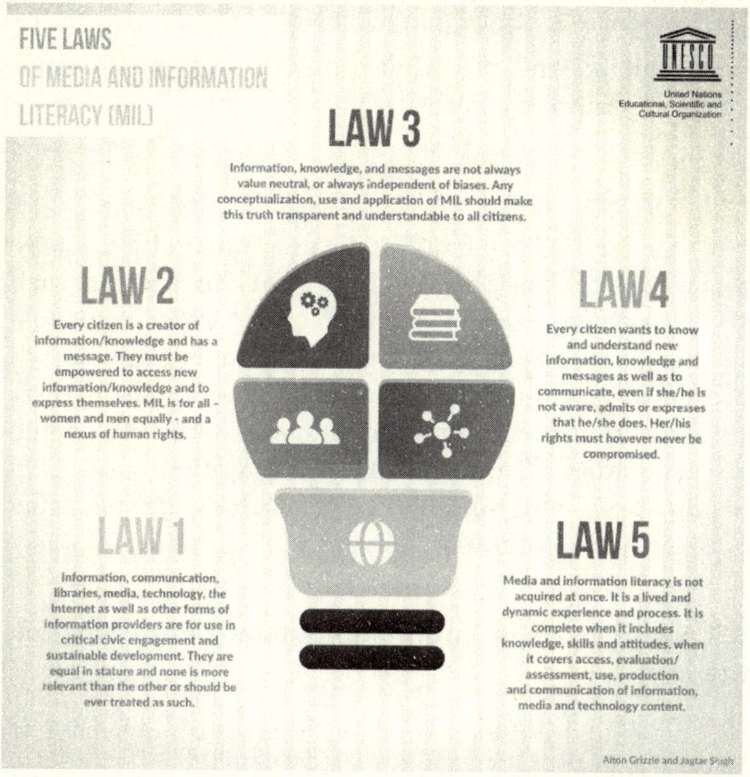

Fig. 9.1. Five Laws of Media and Information Literacy (UNESCO, 2017)

Hypothetically these laws are reflected in the form of core competencies that not only helpful to find information but also to manage and navigate the information from the sea of information/e-information. Thus useful in government, private and public sector to design and execute media and information literacy policies and further initiatives addressed towards super dissemination of information. "Empowerment of people through Media and Information Literacy (MIL) is an important prerequisite for fostering equitable access to information and knowledge and promoting free, independent and pluralistic media and information systems" (Sammongkol, 2017).

9.2. Skill Fair

Under the line of Skill India program (in India) there is need to establish 'Skill Lab' and 'Skill Fair' to strengthen skill based learning as a counter part of e-learning module so that more emphasis is given on practical and design aspects for the individuals to utilize maximum use of their skills and competencies for their innovative tasks. Opening of Community Library and Information Centers (CLIC) at rural areas will work as a backbone for wide spreading of concept of information literacy.

9.3. Significance of information literacy/e-information literacy

Suriya (2009) has mentioned the importance of information literacy in following lines:

- "Global competition/new economic order
- Information explosion, free flow of information and information overload
- Birth of interdisciplinary subjects, fusion and fission of subjects
- Revolution of Information and Communication Technology (ICT)
- Availability of information sources in various media/formats/places
- Thrust and need for research on all fields for socio-economic development

- Thrust for publishing papers
- Web has become the preferred media for publication
- Access methods and Information retrieval tools and techniques
- Security and privacy in the networked environment
- Reliability and accuracy of information and IPR and Copyright issues
- Growth of educational institutions across the globe"

Further for the promotion and wide spread network of information literacy, UNESCO is celebrating 'United Nations Literacy Decade (2003-2012) by its contemporary programs like 'Education for All Program' (EFAP) and the 'Information for All Program (IFAP) for benefit of all.

It is obvious from the above factors that information literacy is a survival skill, which one should needs to acquire.

9.3.1. The merits of information literacy at different levels are mentioned below-

- Systematic searching/accessing technique of print/ web/CD-ROM resources by filtering/ sub-filtering/ refining mechanism and classification of resources, helps to provide personalized services like Selective Dissemination of information (SDI) or Current Awareness Service (CAS) ;
- It provides opportunities to make effective, efficient and independent use of information resources and services as easy-to-use technology of e-information;
- Support in Open Distance Learning (ODL) surroundings;

- Acts as a Meta learning module in the teaching-learning process;
- Serve as an assessment criteria (standard) of accreditation/reaccreditation of colleges/universities and incorporate space for feedback of user's comments, corrections and criticism;
- Awareness and availability of different information systems and technology through networking;
- Scope towards e-courses like electronic learning (e-learning) and blended learning (b-learning) as well as towards independent learning, research, extension activities and learning commons;
- It respects the ownership of information in the digital scenario and support for ethical use of information and control over Digital Rights Management (DRM)/ access rights and legal issues as use of information literacy skills and standards;
- Exploring about e-content and e-information service, its use and application which helps the learners to create awareness to accept the change resulting into a resourceful personality;
- Help the users to take relevant informed judgments and decisions by exploring deception and disinformation;
- Workforce preparation which demands for problem solving skills;
- User will be able to locate/access library holdings through their own networked desktop from their department/laboratory/home by knowing link to web sources in their discipline e.g. e-journals, open archives, Subject gateways etc. ;

- Help in e-governance project by spreading information awareness in rural areas;
- Succeed in resource based learning oriented environment;
- Serve as a motivating factor towards self-directed learning and appreciation towards lifelong learning;
- Methodical synthesis of data, information into knowledge ; and
- Help to develop Civic environment.

9.4. CONCLUSION

From the above, it is clear that Information Literacy/ e-information literacy has been widely discussed and strongly recommended by educational institutions, professional organizations, management centers and experts. It is need of the hour that LIS professionals need to improve their information literacy skills for self as well as for users' development as information is the primary resource instead of capital and labour in today's knowledge economy. Various information literacy models and standards like ACRL, SCONUL etc are best suited to handle and apply on today's e-information literacy programmes. The stated information, methods and practicing skills mentioned are loudly useful for searching the desired information rather than depending on traditional cumbersome process which may evolve the term 'Information Literacy 2.0/3.0'.

UNESCO initiated to bring Information Literacy and Media literacy i.e MIL at a single platform so that all forms of media and sources of information provider rest at common place where combined set of skills and competencies are functional for better access and retrieval of information for the benefit of individuals.

Looking into the significance of information literacy it was decided to include 'Information Literacy' component in each UG/PG course of the LIS curriculum by Government of Maharashtra. This is as per the directives given in JBVC, University Librarians met in the state.

REFERENCES

1. Sammongkol, Nuttavut. Retrieved from http://www.unesco.org/new/en/communication-and-information/capacity-building-tools/media-and-information-literacy/

2. Suriya, M., & others (2009, January-March). Essential information literacy skills of LIS professionals in engineering institutions based on ACRL standards: Need of a study, *SALIS Journal of Library and Information Science*, 1(1), 26-33.

3. Unesco, Retrieved from http://www.unesco.org/new/en/communication-and-information/media-development/media-literacy/five-laws-of-mil/

Bibliography

1. Abraham, A. & Dubey, J. P. (2013, April-June). The road to literacy: a reality check, *Indian journal of adult education*, 74 (2), 73-84.

2. American Library Association (1989). *Presidential Committee on Information Literacy*. Final Report. Chicago: American Library Association.

3. Anderson, Tony & Johnston Bill (2017, March), *Critical Thinking, Information Literacy and Epistemological Development: a Webinar*, Views on Information Literacy in Librarianship, Elsevier and Chandos Webinar Series Retrieved from http://scitechconnect.elsevier.com/wp-content/uploads/2017/03/Information-Literacy-Webinar-3-14-final.pdf

4. Association of College and Research Libraries (2000). *Information Literacy Competency Standards for Higher Education*. Retrieved from www.ala.org/ala/acrl/acrlstandards.htm

5. Association of College and Research Libraries (2014). *Framework for Information Literacy for Higher Education* Retrieved from http://acrl.ala.org/ilstandards/?page_id=133

6. Barry, C. A. (1997, June), Information skills for an electronic world: training doctoral research students, *Journal of information science*, 23(3), 225-228.

7. Baskaran, C. (2011, October 10-16). Information Literacy expertise: a preliminary technique on knowledge accomplishment in academic society. *University News* 49(41), 6-10.

8. Big 6, Retrieved from www.big6.com/pages/about/big6-skills-overview.php

9. Bilawar Prakash B, & Pujar S.M (2011, March 2-4), *Information Literacy Models: Correlation and Conceptual Model for Higher Education*. Proceedings of 8th International CALIBER – 2011 sponsored by INFLIBNET Center, Goa: Goa University.

10. Bilawar Prakash Bhairu (2015, July). Role of working organizations in promotion of Information Literacy initiatives in India, *Vishwawarana National Research Journal*, 2 (2), 6-9.

11. Bose, G. (2010, July-September). Web bases planning and monitoring information system, *Saakshar bharat newsletter*, 6 (8), 46.

12. Bowden, R. (2005, October 3-7), *Information skills for learning*, Part II. In Empowering 8. Proceedings of International Workshop sponsored by IFLA-ALP and UNESCO-IFAP, Patiala: Punjabi University.

13. British Library (2008). *A Ciber briefing paper, information behavior of the researcher of the future.* London: Ciber, British Library.

14. Bruce, C. (1997). *The seven faces of information literacy*. Adelaide: Auslib Press.

15. Bruce, C. (2003). *Seven faces of information literacy:*

Towards inviting students into new experiences. QUT, Retrieved from http://kennison.name/files/zopestore/uploads/libraries/bruce-7-faces.pdf

16. Campbell, D. (2000). Australian subject gateways: Political and strategic issues. *Online information review*, 24 (1), 73-77.

17. Cassidy, S, & Eachus, P. (1998). *Developing the computer self-efficacy(CSE) scale: investigating the relationship between CSE, gender and experience with computers* Retrieved from www.chssc.salford.ac.uk/healthSci/ selfeff/selfeff.htm.

18. Chaminda, C. J. (2008). User perceptions and expectations on e-information literacy development programmes: a gap analysis. *ORBIS-Scientific e-journal of Human Science,* 4 (10).

19. Chartered Institute of Library and Information Professionals (2012), *Information Literacy Skills* Retrieved from http://www.cilip.org.uk/sites/ default/files/documents/Information%20literacy%20skills.pdf

20. CMIE (1994, August). Economic Intelligence Service, *Basic Statics India.* CMIE.

21. Cook D. & Sittler, R. L. (2008). *Practical pedagogy for Library Instructors: 17 Innovative Strategies to improve student learning*, USA: American Library Association.

22. Coravu, R. (2010, April 21-23). Library literacy: the step before information literacy, *First international conference in Romanian on Information Literacy*, E-Lis: Romania.

23. Corrall, S. (1998, Winter), Key skills for students in higher education, *SCONUL Newsletter*, 15, 25-29.

24. Cox, C. N. (2008). *Information literacy instruction handbook*, Chicago: Association of College and Research Libraries.

25. Crawford, J. & Irving, C. (2009, March). Information Literacy in the workplace: a qualitative exploratory study, *Journal of Librarianship and Information Science*, 41(1), 29-38.

26. Devine, J. & Egger-Sider, F. (2009). *Going beyond Google: The Invisible web in learning and teaching,* London: Facet publishing.

27. Doyle, C.S (1992). *Outcome measure for information literacy within the National Educational Goals of 1990. Final report to the National Forum on Information Literacy.* Syracuse NY: ERIC Clearinghouse on information resources.

28. Educational Testing Service (2007). *Digital transformation: a framework for ICT Literacy, A report of the international ICT literacy panel,* USA: Educational Testing Service, 1-42.

29. Gerber, R. (1998). How do workers learn in the workplace?, *Journal of workplace learning,*16 (1-2), 22-33.

30. Godwin, P. (2005, December). Making life easier for academics: how librarians can help staff weather the technological storm, *Journal of eLiteracy,* 2 (2), 68-79.

31. Godwin, P. & Parker, Jo. (2008). *Information Literacy meets Library 2.0,* London: Facet publishing.

32. Halder, S. N. (2013). *Library and Information Science in Changing Paradigm.* New Delhi: Ess Ess Publications.

33. Horton, F. W. (2009). Information literacy and learning to learn, In Jagtar Singh, etal. (Ed.) *Library and Information Science in Digital Age,* Essays in honor of Professor M.P. Satija, V.1, New Delhi: Ess Ess Publication. P-117-119.

34. India (2012). Retrieved from http:/www.indianchild.com/population.html/

35. Inflibnet, Retrieved from www.inflibnet.ac.in

36. Jain, S. (2011, October 10-16). Inclusion of ICTs in higher education: Technology literacy for today and tomorrow, *University News* V.49 (41), 11-16.

37. Johnson, A. M. (2008). Analogical storytelling as a strategy for teaching concept attainment, In Cook Douglas and Sittler Rayan L. *Practical pedagogy for Library Instructors: 17 Innovative Strategies to improve student learning,* USA: American Library Association.

38. Katz, I. R., & Macklin, A.S. (2007). Information and Communication Technology (ICT) Literacy: Integration and assessment in higher education. *Systemics, Cybernetics and Informatics,* 5(4), 50-55.

39. Khan, K. M & Naika, R. (2010, January 18-19). *Information literacy in promoting information services and empowering professionals in digital era,* UGC sponsored national level conference, Mangalore: St. Agnes College, 389-395.

40. Kilic-Cakmak, E. (2010). Learning strategies and motivational factors predicting information literacy self-efficacy of e-learners, *Australasian Journal of Educational Technology,* 26(2), 192-208.

41. Kishore A. & Padmaja, M. (2013). Information Literacy skills of the PG students towards the use

of electronic information resources: a case study of SVIMS library, Tirupati, In Ramesha Babu (Ed.), *Libraries in the Changing Dimensions of Digital Technology*, Festschrift in honor of Prof. D. Chandran, Delhi: B. R. Publishing Corporation.

42. Konappa, D. (2013). Digital Information Literacy among research scholars in Sri Venkateshwara University, Tirupati (A.P): An analytical study. In Ramesha Babu (Ed.), *Libraries in the Changing Dimensions of Digital Technology*, Festschrift in honour of Prof. D. Chandran, Delhi: B. R. Publishing Corporation.

43. Kumar, P.S.G. (2004). *A Student's Manual of Library and Information Science*, New Delhi: B.R. Publishing Corporation.

44. Kurbanoglu, S.S, Akkoyunlu, B. & Umay, A. (2006). Developing the information literacy self-efficacy scale. *Journal of Documentation,* 62 (6), 730-743.

45. Leon, A. & Leon, M. (2004). *Introduction to information systems.* Chennai: Vijay Nicole imprints private limited.

46. Lihitkar, S. A. A., & Lihitkar, R. S. (2009, July) Models of information literacy. *Information age*, 3 (3), 29-32.

47. Lupton, M. (2004). *The learning connection: Information literacy and the student experience.* Adelaide: Auslib Press.

48. Mahapatra, G. (2006, February 2-4). 'Towards e-information literacy: quest for interoperable web based information system', *4th International Convention CALIBER-2006,* Gulbarga: INFLIBNET Centre, Ahmedabad.

49. Maitaouthong, T. & others (2012, April). The roles of university libraries in supporting the integration of information literacy in the course instruction, *Malaysian Journal of Library & Information Science*, 17 (1), 51-64.

50. Mitchell, E. & Hiatt, D. (2010, November) Perspectives on...Using POGIL Techniques in an Information Literacy Curriculum, *The Journal of Academic Librarianship,* 36 (6), 539–542.

51. Myburgh, S. (2005). *The new Information Professional: how to thrive in the information age doing what you love.* England: Chandos Publishing.

52. National Forum on Information Literacy. (1998). *A Progress Report on Information Literacy: An Update on the American Library Association Presidential Committee on Information Literacy*: Final Report, Chicago.

53. Nayak, V.D. & others (2006, February 2-4). 'E-information literacy: an overview', *4th International Convention CALIBER-2006,* Gulbarga: INFLIBNET Centre, Ahmedabad.

54. Picard, C. J. (2004, January). *Guidelines for Library Media Programs In Louisiana Schools*, Louisiana State Department of Education, Retrieved from http://www.louisianaschools.net/lde/uploads/15303.pdf

55. Pinto, M. (2008, April). Cyberabstracts: a portal on the subject of abstracting designed to improve information literacy skills, *Journal of Information Science* 34 (5), 667-679.

56. Pintrich, P.R. & others (1991). *A manual for the use of the motivated strategies for learning.* Michigan:

The University of Michigan.

57. Pujar, S.M. (2014). Search strategies for effective search on the Internet In Festschrift in honor of Dr. N. I. Divatankar, *Parameters and perspectives of LIS education*, Varanasi: ABS publication.

58. Rai, R. & Dvivedi, S. (2010, August 9-15). Concept Mapping as a technological tool to facilitate teacher education programme and enhance e-learning, *University News*, 48 (32), 14-17.

59. Ramana, Y. V. (2005, January 27-29). *Status of e-learning in India*, 23rd Annual convention and conference SIS-2005, Andhra University, Vishakhapatnam.

60. Ramesh, B., & Ramesha. (2008). Soft skills for library and information science (LIS) professionals in the knowledge society, In Festschrift of Professor C.R. Karisiddappa, *Library and Information Science Profession in the Knowledge Society*, New Delhi: Allied publishers Pvt. Ltd.

61. Sammongkol, Nuttavut. Retrieved from http://www.unesco.org/new/en/communication-and-information/capacity-building-tools/media-and-information-literacy/

62. Secker, J., & others (2007). *The Information Literacy Cookbook: Ingredients, recipes and tips for success*, Great Britain: Chandos Publishing (Oxford) Limited.

63. Senthilkumaran, P. (2011, June). Information literacy Programs in India, *SRELS Journal of Information Management*. 48 (3), 357-363.

64. Slavin, R. E. (2006). *Educational Psychology: Theory and practice*, Boston: Pearson.

65. Society of College, National and University libraries (1999). *The seven pillars of information literacy*, Retrieved from http://www.sconul.ac.uk/activities/inf lit/papers/seven pillars.html

66. Society of College, National and University libraries (2011, April). *The SCONUL seven pillars of information literacy, SCONUL working group on Information Literacy*, Retrieved from http:// www.sconul.ac.uk/sites/default/ files/documents/ coremodel.pdf

67. Society of College, National and University libraries (2004). *Learning Outcomes and Information Literacy*, London: Higher Education Academy.

68. Suriya, M., & others (2009, January-March). Essential information literacy skills of LIS professionals in engineering institutions based on ACRL standards: Need of a study, *SALIS Journal of Library and Information Science*, 1(1), 26-33.

69. Tiwari, P. (2009). *Library Evaluation*, New Delhi: APH Publishing Corporation.

70. Unesco, Retrieved from http://www.unesco.org/new/en/communication-and-information/media-development/media-literacy/five-laws-of-mil/

71. Uribe, T. A. (2009). Interrelaciones entre veinte definiciones-descripciones del concepto de alfabetización informacional: propuesta de macro-definición. ACIMED. Revista cubana de los profesionales de la información y de la comunicación en salud, 20, n. (Spanish) In Tirado, Alejandro Uribe, Information Literacy Competency Standards for Higher Education and their Correlation with the Cycle of Knowledge Generation, *Liber Quarterly*, 22 (3), 2012.

72. Walsh, A. (2009, March). Information literacy assessment: Where do we start?, *Journal of Librarianship and Information Science*, 41(1), 19-28.

73. Wijayasundara, N. D. (2008). Faculty-library collaboration: A model for University of Colombo, *The International Information and Library Review*, 40, 188-198.

74. Zurkowski, P. G. (1974). *The Information Service Environment Relationships and Priorities,* Related Paper No. 5, National Commission on Libraries and Information Science, Washington, DC: National Program for Library and Information Services. Retrieved from http://eric.ed.gov/PDFS/ED100391.pdf